PEGGY FLANAGAN

Ogimaa Kwe, Lieutenant Governor

JESSICA ENGELKING

MINNESOTA NATIVE AMERICAN LIVES SERIES

ISBN 13: 978-1-63489-366-4
Library of Congress Catalog Number: 2020913756
Printed in the United States of America
First Printing: 2020

24 23 22 21 20   5 4 3 2 1

Illustrations © 2020 Tashia Hart
Book design by Patrick Maloney
Back cover photo: Courtesy State of Minnesota, www.mn.gov/governor/about/peggyflanagan

This work is funded with money from the Arts and Cultural Heritage Fund that was created with the vote of the people of Minnesota on November 4, 2008.

 Minnesota
Humanities
Center

  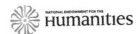

Wise Ink Creative Publishing
807 Broadway St. NE, Suite 46
Minneapolis, MN 55413
wiseink.com

To order, visit itascabooks.com or call 1-800-901-3480. Reseller discounts available.

CONTENTS

INTRODUCTION

S torytelling is a traditional tool of many Indigenous people, and here in Minnesota our storytelling tradition is alive and well among Native Americans of many nations. The authors, illustrators, and editors of this series, who are all Dakota or Ojibwe, continue their cultural traditions in creating these books.

The Minnesota Humanities Center and the editors of this series of books for younger readers believe it is important to envision the future through stories of the past and present. Our goal is to help Native American children see their cultures represented alongside biographies of other leaders in our larger society. We envisioned a series of children's books by, for, and about Dakota and Anishinaabe (Ojibwe) and other Indigenous people, portraying our histories, knowledge ways, culture keepers, and beloved figures. These biographies are meant to help Dakota, Anishinaabe, and other Native American children imagine their own potential for full futures.

Of all the children's books published in the United States, only 1 percent are written by Native and First Nations authors, according to the Cooperative Children's Book Center at the University of Wisconsin–Madison.[1]

Our hope is that teachers and parents will encourage young readers

---

1 Data on books by and about people from First/Native Nations published for children and teens compiled by the Cooperative Children's Book Center, School of Education, University of Wisconsin–Madison. ccbc.education.wisc.edu/books/pcstats.asp

to see themselves in the extraordinary lives presented in these stories. We also hope readers will consider how the facts of social barriers based in race, culture, education, and class influenced the lives of the subjects of these books. History, especially the impacts of treaties, underlies these stories as well. These are narratives that open up contexts of language and culture and the policies meant to destroy them. The legacy of boarding schools and forced education away from family figures into each story to some extent. Poverty and the disruption of family life are also themes too many children can relate to, and the women and men featured in these narratives overcame just such circumstances.

The first books in this series include stories of historic figures who lived, worked, and broke barriers a hundred years ago, as well as the ongoing story of an exceptional Ojibwe woman who rose to the highest levels of leadership in Minnesota and in the nation.

—Gwen Nell Westerman and Heid E. Erdrich,
series editors, May 2020

Chapter One

NO MORE PAPER HEADDRESSES

St. Louis Park, MN
1986

Peggy Flanagan can hear her name being called.

"Peggy, come on!" her friends yell. They are trying to get enough kids together for a game of Red Rover. Peggy hurries over to where they are gathering. Recess is more fun when they play together like this. They pick teams and form two lines facing each other. They link arms and Peggy's team goes first.

"Red rover, red rover!" they shout together. The team Peggy is on calls over a boy Peggy doesn't know very well. He sits in the same row of desks as her and seems nice enough. He runs over and tries to break through the middle. He almost makes it, but they're able to stop him. He joins Peggy's team and they wait for the other team to call someone over.

Peggy likes her classmates. She is in first grade and goes to school in St. Louis Park, Minnesota. St. Louis Park is a suburb of Minneapolis. The schools in St. Louis Park are really good. That's why Peggy and her mom moved there. Peggy's school is pretty diverse, but there aren't many kids who are Native American, like Peggy. Peggy is Ojibwe on her father's side. Her mom is raising Peggy on her own, so Peggy doesn't know much about the Ojibwe side of her family.

After a few more rounds of Red Rover, Peggy is pretty sure the other side is going to call her over next. She is right.

"Red rover, red rover, send PEGGY right over!" the team yells.

Peggy is small and with her asthma, she can't always run fast. The other team is confident she won't be able to break through their linked arms. Peggy isn't a quitter. She digs her sneakers into the grass and charges toward the row of kids.

"Oof!" She doesn't break through. Peggy joins hands with her new teammates and the game continues. Peggy enjoys being outside for recess. She needs a break from the classroom. Earlier in the day, they had been talking about Native Americans in Peggy's class. Peggy doesn't like the way they are taught about Native Americans. She doesn't like how the whole class will turn to look at her, because she is the only Native American in the room. Peggy doesn't like how they are taught that Christopher Columbus discovered America. She doesn't think it makes sense to say someone discovered a place when there's already people living there. Peggy's Ojibwe ancestors were here long before Columbus. Besides, Columbus did a lot of bad things, but they don't talk about those. He doesn't seem like the kind of person who should have his own holiday, but he does. The way the class talks about Natives in the past tense bothers Peggy too. It makes it seem like Natives don't exist. It makes Peggy feel like she's not supposed to exist.

"FWEET!!!" Peggy snaps back to attention. The whistle means recess is over. Kids start heading over to where they are supposed to line up. Peggy walks over to get in line with the rest of her class. She isn't excited to go back inside. It is nice outside. Also, Peggy is pretty sure they are going to continue their unit on Native Americans when they get back into the classroom.

The students walk in two lines back to their classroom and go sit down at their desks. Peggy's teacher tells the class to open their books and turn to the part about the first Thanksgiving. Like a lot of Native kids, Peggy has mixed feelings about Thanksgiving. Even though the food is good and it's nice to have the time off from school, Thanksgiving sometimes feels fake. It doesn't really seem like people are thankful for Native Americans today. It seems like people just see Natives as sports team mascots or the bad guys in old movies. There's even a football team that has a bad word for Native people for its name. So Peggy doesn't feel like people are really thankful for the Native people who took care of the first settlers. If they did, they wouldn't treat living Natives the way they do. There is one thing Peggy is thankful for: at least they are not making paper headdresses in class. Some classes have students make fake feather headdresses to wear. It makes Peggy sad to see kids wearing headdresses made out of construction paper and staples. It makes her feel like being Native is something you pretend to be, not something you really are.

Peggy tries to keep her head down for the rest of the day. She doesn't feel like being a part of class today. When they talk about Native Americans, Peggy just feels confused. She knows that what they are taught about Natives Americans, if not wrong, at least doesn't tell the whole truth. But Peggy herself doesn't really know what the whole truth is. She has a lot of questions. There's a lot she is unsure about. She hopes one day she will find some answers.

Chapter Two

"WHAT ARE YOU?"

St. Louis Park, MN
1988

Nine-year-old Peggy Flanagan isn't a psychic, but she knows exactly what the lady's second question will be: "No, I mean *where are you from?*" Peggy had been getting groceries with her mother and wandered off on her own to explore the aisles of the supermarket. And that's when the lady approached her with a curious look on her face. Peggy knows this look. It means this lady is about to come up to Peggy and start asking her questions. The lady is getting closer. A few more steps and . . . Peggy braces herself.

"Hello, umm, I'm sorry, but I just *have* to ask—" (*No*, thought Peggy, *you really don't.*) "What are you?"

Peggy knows what the lady is getting at. She wants to know Peggy's race or ethnicity. She wants to know why Peggy looks different from white kids. Peggy doesn't think she looks *that* different. She has chin-length brown hair (cute headband, of course) and brown eyes. But her skin is just a little bit darker, and her features are a little bit unfamiliar to some people. Which is why the lady asked, *What are you?*

"A person . . . ?" Peggy replies. She lets her answer trail off into a question. Did the lady want to keep going with this, or would she get the hint that it was an inappropriate question?

"No, I mean *where are you from?*"

"I am Ojibwe." Peggy knows it will go faster if she just gives the lady what she wants. But the woman gives Peggy another questioning look.

"Did you say 'Jewish'?" the lady asks, uncertain what she had heard.

"No," Peggy says. "I said Ojibwe. I'm Native American." Now Peggy sees a look of recognition on the lady's face. A look like, "Oh, Native American! I have heard of your people!" Peggy knows the lady has gotten the answer she wanted. Now she can leave, satisfied she discovered a Native child roaming wild in the aisles of Red Owl.

"Oh, how interesting!" the lady says before walking away, as if their interaction never happened. Just like that. To the lady, it was an exotic encounter. To Peggy, it was a sad reminder that she looked different from other kids. It was a reminder that people noticed she wasn't entirely like them.

Peggy doesn't really know what it means to be Ojibwe—yet. Peggy's father is Ojibwe, a member of the White Earth Nation, and so is Peggy. But she doesn't know much about her father or his family. She hasn't even met him yet. Peggy's mom has raised her on her own. She knows her father is Ojibwe and she is Ojibwe and that is a connection they share. But Peggy doesn't feel fully connected to the Native part of herself. It feels like something's missing.

Peggy and her mom are getting ready to check out at the grocery store. Peggy always dreads this part, just a little bit. She just doesn't want to end up having to see *the look*. Peggy's mom uses food stamps to buy groceries for the family. Some people judge Peggy and her mom for this. Sometimes the look is pity—they look at Peggy and her mom like they feel sorry for them. Sometimes it's anger—some people think people on food stamps are lazy. But Peggy's mom works harder than anyone Peggy has ever met. Sometimes people just want to feel better than someone else. No matter the reason, Peggy doesn't like the look. But Peggy and her mom are in luck. No one is in line when Peggy's mom tears out the colorful rectangular vouchers from her booklet and hands them to the cashier.

It is the same way at school too. Peggy's lunch tickets are a different color. There are different colors for full-price, reduced-price, and free lunches, so everyone can see who the poor kids are. It is embarrassing for Peggy. Even though she knows it is pointless, Peggy still tries to hide her ticket. She'll palm it like a card trick, tuck it in her shoe, or find another way to avoid being obviously different. Peggy still wasn't sure why she felt embarrassed about it. The other kids hadn't done anything other than be born to wealthy parents. But that was enough for them to see themselves as better than Peggy.

When they get home, Peggy helps her mom put away the groceries. Her mom starts dinner and Peggy finishes up her last bit of homework. Peggy is still thinking about her encounter at the store. That lady definitely recognized the term "Native American," but Peggy was pretty sure her idea of Native Americans is all wrong. She probably thought Peggy lived in a teepee or something.

This lady is not alone. A lot of people think this way. People believe what they are shown, and they're not shown Natives like Peggy. They see "Cowboys and Indians" and sports team mascots. Peggy doesn't see anyone like her in the movies or on the news. Or in books or in front of the classroom. Or politics or most places.

It's sort of the same with being poor. People are given the idea that people on assistance are lazy and taking their hard-earned money from them. But that's not true. Peggy's mom works so hard, but without the food stamps, they just wouldn't have enough healthy food on the table. Peggy is grateful for these programs. She is grateful to have a mom who does everything she can for Peggy. It can be a struggle at times, but she is happy. It's Peggy and her mom against the world.

Chapter Three

KEEPING BUSY

St. Louis Park High School
1994

P eggy keeps looking at the clock. Ten minutes to go. Then five minutes. Then one minute. Peggy starts to gather her things. Any moment now, they would announce it.

"Speech students are dismissed!" Peggy's teacher calls out. Peggy quickly and quietly exits the classroom. It is fun getting to leave class early. Their speech meet isn't too far away, so they were really only missing the last half hour of the school day. They had gotten whatever homework they would be missing in advance. Peggy heads to her locker to grab her jacket and backpack, then she makes her way to the doors where they were to wait for the bus.

The bus is there already, waiting for them. They file on and each student claims a seat. There are more bus seats than speech students, so everyone has a seat to themselves. Peggy cracks a window. She isn't sure if this bus driver is okay with them opening windows. The driver doesn't say anything, so Peggy figures it's all right to get some fresh air.

The kids who are able to read without getting carsick read over their prepared pieces and notes. Peggy knows the ride will be over soon enough and decides to use this time to just relax. She balls up her coat into a makeshift pillow and wedges it between the seat and the window. Peggy tries to get comfortable. At least she isn't very tall. Peggy feels bad for her tall friends when she sees them scrunched up in their seats.

Peggy is pretty tired. She hasn't been sleeping well. Peggy's step-dad is violent and she doesn't always feel safe at home. Peggy's mom married him when Peggy was ten. Peggy and her mom moved up the street into a white house on the corner with Peggy's stepdad and his children. It isn't far from Peggy's old place, but it feels like a world away. Now she isn't comfortable at home, and she does whatever she can to avoid being there. Extracurriculars like speech are a great way to avoid being at the house.

It was Mr. Redman's idea for Peggy to join speech. He thought she would be good at it. It makes Peggy feel good to have a teacher like Mr. Redman. He believes in her, and he understands aspects of her life that other teachers do not. Mr. Redman is a Black man. He knows what it is like to stand out among a sea of white faces. It's not that Peggy's other teachers are racist; they just don't see Peggy being Ojibwe as relevant. But Mr. Redman, and a few other teachers of color, understand that it matters. It affects the way the world treats Peggy. Mr. Redman encouraged Peggy to join speech because he knew the world wouldn't strain to hear what she has to say. Peggy's voice needed to be loud and clear.

Before Peggy knows it, the bus pulls into the parking lot, joining a small handful of other buses from nearby schools. Peggy remains seated. She's not in a hurry to get off the bus. Her event isn't first, so she doesn't have to rush to get ready. Sometimes Peggy thinks it's funny that she's in speech because there are times when Peggy just can't find the words she needs.

She's speechless an awful lot for someone who competes in speech. Peggy isn't sure if the words are there and she can't find them, or if

maybe the words she's looking for don't even exist. Whenever she tries to describe the hole she feels inside, Peggy doesn't have the words. "Hole" isn't even the right word, but it's the best word Peggy has to describe it. Holes have sides and a bottom. What Peggy feels has no defined shape. It just feels *empty*. Sometimes when people lose an arm or a leg, they feel a phantom pain where the limb used to be. That's how Peggy feels sometimes, except it is a piece of her soul or something that feels missing.

Peggy makes her way off the bus. She is ready to support her fellow teammates and cheer them on. Peggy isn't sure if she's going to do well today, but she will try her hardest. More than winning, Peggy wants to make Mr. Redman proud. He believes in her, and Peggy at least owes it to him, and herself, to give it her very best.

Chapter Four

MR. REDMAN'S ROOM

St. Louis Park High School
1997

t feels like all the air has gone out of the room. Peggy can't breathe. As scary as it is, it is not an unfamiliar feeling. Peggy's asthma is pretty bad. She'd even been hospitalized a couple times when she was younger.

But this isn't her asthma. It is a feeling of shock. It is fear. It is panic and confusion. Peggy slumps into a seat, grateful she has Mr. Redman's classroom to take a moment in. She feels completely lost. What is happening doesn't seem entirely real. Peggy sits alone in Mr. Redman's classroom, asking herself the most difficult question she's ever had to ask herself: "Am I dumb?"

Peggy looks down at the report card in her hands. It still didn't seem real. She would be graduating, *barely*, with a 1.75 grade point average. That's really bad. So bad that Peggy has to actually ask herself the painful question, "Am I dumb?" That would explain her academic performance. Peggy doesn't want to be dumb. But looking at the report card she is holding and seeing her 1.75 GPA, dumb is exactly how Peggy feels. She feels like a failure.

It's not like she does horribly in *all* her classes. Peggy does okay in some of them, like Mr. Redman's. But for the most part, she isn't interested in her classes. She doesn't want to be there. She isn't engaged, so she doesn't really try.

"Or," worried Peggy, "maybe that's just what I'm telling myself. Maybe I'm just dumb." But there are definitely people who believe in Peggy, like her mom and teachers like Mr. Redman. They don't think she is dumb. Still, Peggy can't shake the worry that she doesn't measure up. Looking at her report card, Peggy's academic performance has earned her a score of 1.75 out of 4.0. That is not good.

Peggy does well with other aspects of school, though. By the end of high school, Peggy has mastered the art of extracurricular activities. She does speech, show choir, and theater. She has been elected to the student council. She's even the editor in chief of the high school's literary arts magazine. Peggy *loves* writing. Writing is an escape. It got her through some tough times when she was younger. Peggy loves being so involved. Not only does it get her out of the house, but it allows her to hang out with great people. Peggy is totally a theater kid. A part of her is a natural storyteller. And Peggy loves spending time with other theater kids. They are clever and exciting and a little weird, and they make Peggy feel accepted.

Peggy sighs. Taking one last look at her report card, Peggy can't even believe she's been accepted to college. But she'll be starting at St. Cloud State University in the fall. Peggy is so ready to be done with high school. There are some things, like the safety of Mr. Redman's room, that she will miss, though. When Peggy is in Mr. Redman's room, she feels like it is okay not to have things figured out. It's okay to have questions about who she is. And Peggy has a lot of questions.

Chapter Five

THE WRITING ON THE WALL

St. Cloud State University
St. Cloud, MN
1998

Peggy sees the paper taped to her door. It's happened again. Someone left a photocopy of a Native mascot and some gross language on Peggy's dorm room door.

Peggy rips it down and crumples it into a ball. It wasn't even worth bothering to save it to show somebody. This had been going on for a while. Peggy had shown similar notes to the people at her college whom she thought could help her. And nothing happened. They knew who was doing it too, yet they did nothing. There wasn't much left of the school year, so even if they did, it wouldn't really matter at this point anyway.

When Peggy left home for college at St. Cloud State University, she had not anticipated this. St. Cloud is only an hour north of St. Louis Park on Interstate 94. But it felt noticeably different. There's racism against Natives everywhere, but the environment Peggy found herself in was more aggressively racist than she'd ever experienced. It's not like there wasn't racism in St. Louis Park. But despite there being only one (ONE!) other Native in Peggy's class, it was a relatively diverse student body. For the most part, everyone hung out and got along, no matter who they were. That wasn't the vibe Peggy was getting at SCSU. People seemed to be isolated in groups.

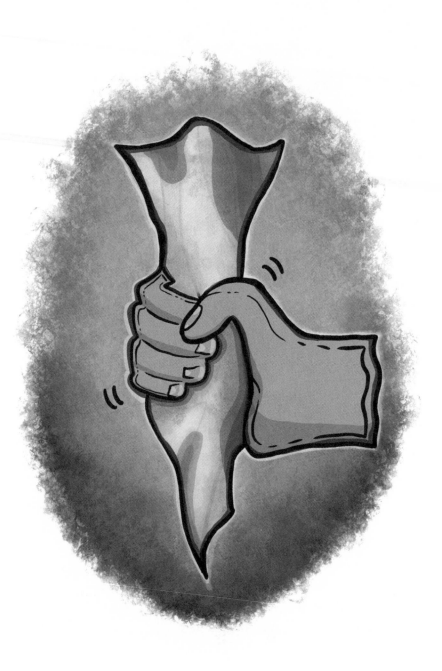

Peggy is a bit distracted by the racist poster and fumbles getting her key into the lock. Finally, she hears it click. It had been a long and, other than the door thing, pretty awesome day. Peggy absolutely loves concert choir rehearsal. St. Cloud State has a good concert choir. Peggy is really getting into her musical education. Concert choir was one of the main reasons she chose St. Cloud State. She probably wouldn't even be there if not for the choir. So much of what made the choir great is its director. He is a really good choir director. Peggy knew she was lucky to get to study under him. And she knows her luck has run out.

Peggy flips on the light and flops on her dorm room's twin bed. She has a big decision to make. Recently, Peggy's choir director had dropped a huge announcement. "I'm taking a job in Michigan," he said. He'd gotten a job offer from a university there and would be moving. He is the reason why Peggy is at SCSU. His leaving threw everything for a loop.

"You can follow me, if you want," the choir director had said to Peggy. It was a nice offer and reassuring to have at least one option for transfer. Peggy needs to get out of St. Cloud. Now that her reason for being there is gone, there isn't any point in staying. In addition to the invitation to Michigan, Peggy's choir director offered her another alternative.

"Why don't you consider transferring to the University of Minnesota?" he suggested. Peggy's choir director seemed to think the U of M would be a good place for her. It would be a healthier environment. He could put her in touch with the choir there.

Peggy decides to take his advice. The U of M is a great university, and it'd be nice to be back in the metro area. Peggy is grateful that this transfer is going through. She is still haunted by that 1.75 GPA she graduated with. But for her part, Peggy had taken the classes she needed in order to transfer. And she did well enough in them that the University of Minnesota accepted her application. Peggy knows they are taking a risk. Sometimes all it takes, though, is giving people a chance.

Chapter Six

GUIDING LIGHTS

University of Minnesota
Minneapolis, MN
1999

Not everyone is able to point to a moment and say, "This is a moment that changed my life." Walking into her first class at the University of Minnesota, Peggy was about to have one of those life-changing experiences.

Peggy had experienced a lot of life changes recently. She left St. Cloud to transfer to the University of Minnesota–Twin Cities. She was stepping away from choir as a career. Peggy still loves to sing, but wants to keep it as just that, something she loves doing. She has a lot of feelings as she approaches the building where her first class is taught. It is an Ojibwe class, and Peggy cannot believe she's finally getting to learn about her people. She is finally getting to learn about who she is. But Peggy was not prepared for the feeling she would experience when she entered the classroom. The moment Peggy looked up at the front of the classroom, everything changed. Peggy felt something she had never felt in a classroom before: *she looks like me. She IS like me.*

The person at the front of the classroom, the one who looks like Peggy, is Dr. Brenda Child, a professor at the University of Minnesota. Like Peggy, Dr. Child is Ojibwe, though she is from Red Lake, not White Earth. Peggy can't get enough of her classes with Dr. Child. All of a sudden, Peggy is like a sponge for knowledge. That hole Peggy had felt since high school is suddenly being filled with history and language and culture. It feels amazing. With Dr. Child's guidance, Peggy dives into Ojibwe studies. She starts taking graduate-level courses. She even enrolls in honors courses for fun. (FUN!)

Peggy has another guiding light at the U of M: Professor Dennis Jones. He is Peggy's guide to the cultural aspects of Ojibwe studies. Peggy absolutely loves his classes. She learns so much and at the same time he is so funny! Peggy and her classmates laugh so hard.

It's not just having Native teachers that's new to Peggy. Native classmates are new to Peggy too. Growing up in St. Louis Park, Peggy was used to being the only Native in the classroom. Part of being the only Native in the class means you don't get to experience having Native classmates. Peggy likes her new classmates. She likes the feeling of being around other Ojibwe. A lot of her classmates are funny, like her teacher, Dennis Jones. They take what they are doing seriously. They are respectful. But they also love to joke around. The classroom is often filled with laughter.

Peggy loves to laugh. People who love to laugh are able to find humor almost anywhere. Peggy learned to find humor in some dark places growing up. She suspects that a lot of other Natives are like her in that way. There's a lot of trauma in the Native communities. Boarding schools separated Native children from their families, their languages, and their cultures. Many children were abused. What happened in boarding schools hurt badly, and many people were traumatized, and their trauma spread. But the ability to laugh endured, and laughter helped the healing even in the next generations.

Peggy feels like she is healing. For so long, she felt an emptiness inside of her. Now, she is filling that empty hole with knowledge about herself and her people. She is healing with laughter and learning. She is making connections to the part of herself she had been missing for far too long.

Chapter Seven

CALLED TO SERVE

Little Earth
2017

K*nock, knock.*

Peggy waits to see if anyone will answer. Peggy is knocking on doors to share information important to the citizens of Little Earth. Door-knocking in Little Earth can be tricky, Peggy knows. She's been doing it for over a decade. There wasn't a light on that she could see, but Peggy thought maybe she heard someone moving around inside. When no one comes to the door, Peggy continues to the next. There are lots of unit doors to knock on, and it wouldn't be too long before she'd start losing light.

Little Earth was created in the early 1970s as the first-ever urban housing project with a Native preference for those who lived there. There's probably somewhere between 1,200 and 1,500 people living at Little Earth. It can be hard to keep an exact count. Not everyone living there is listed on a lease. A lot of people take in family, because that's what family does. Still, it was a lot of people for a little over nine acres. An acre is slightly smaller than a football field. While many of the Natives living in the 212 units are Dakota, Lakota, or Ojibwe, there are Natives from dozens of different tribes residing there.

As Peggy moves door to door, she can't help but think of the first time she went door-knocking. During Peggy's senior year at the University of Minnesota, she was in charge of Paul Wellstone's campaign initiative to reach out to Urban Natives. She hadn't started out in that position. Peggy had passed the Wellstone for Senate office many times. She liked the work Senator Wellstone was doing and often thought about stopping in. One day, a day like any other, Peggy heard a little voice telling her to go in. And Peggy listened. She walked into the Wellstone for Senate office and offered to do whatever she could to help. She stuffed envelopes and cleaned up, and before long she was heading up the Urban Native outreach. Urban Natives are a demographic that is often overlooked. But this campaign changed things. Peggy was out there constantly, knocking on doors, listening to what people had to say. She wasn't just out there to tell the people what she wanted them to do. She was listening to them and letting them speak to their needs. Peggy knows that people know their own needs best—it's just a matter of listening to them.

Sadly, the Wellstone campaign came to a tragic end just eleven days before the election. A few minutes past ten on the morning of October 25, 2002, the plane carrying Senator Paul Wellstone, his wife Sheila, their daughter, three campaign staffers, and two pilots crashed in northern Minnesota and everyone aboard died. It was a day of shock and grief across the state. Peggy couldn't believe her first campaign would be Wellstone's last. Senator Wellstone will always be one of her heroes and political inspirations. He was known for saying, "We all do better when we all do better." Peggy believes these words with all her heart.

The loss of Senator Wellstone had hit Peggy hard, but she knew she needed to keep moving forward. As it turned out, moving forward brought her right back to Little Earth. Peggy's former professor, Dr. Brenda Child, helped connect her with a job at the Division of Indian Works (DIW). There she headed its Parents Plus program, bridging the gap between Native families and the school system.

There's a lot of work to be done to improve relations between Native families and the school system. Native families can be wary of the school system. The boarding school days were not that long ago. There's not a lot of trust there.

Something else was missing from schools too: representation. The Minneapolis School Board had never had a Native board member. It was no wonder the Native community was having issues with the school system. They had never been a part of the decision-making process. That's the problem. Well, part of the problem, anyway. Peggy knew if they could get someone to win a seat on the school board, the Native community would be able to speak to their needs. What Peggy didn't know at the time was that someone would be her.

As she hustles to hit up the last few units, Peggy thinks back to the conversations that led up to her running for the Minneapolis School Board.

"You should be the one to do it," they had told her. Peggy remembers not knowing what to say. The thought of saying no to elders felt wrong but, honestly, it was a terrible idea. Peggy had tried to find someone from the Native community to run for a school board. Surely, somebody's auntie knew somebody whose cousin's friend would make a good candidate. Better than Peggy, at least. At the time, Peggy was only twenty-four years old and she didn't even have any kids. What kind of school board candidate is that?

The kind that wins, apparently. Peggy is grateful she listened to the elders when they encouraged her to run. They had called on her to serve, so she did as she was asked. Peggy had stepped up and won the first of many elections. It wasn't about winning, though. It was about being a voice for the people.

It's time to wrap things up at Little Earth. Peggy is done for the evening. As she gets ready to head back to meet with the rest of her crew, she can't help but think about the second time she was caught off guard by a request for her to run for office. It hadn't been that long ago. She clearly remembers the shock of it all.

Chapter Eight

BIG DECISIONS

Little Earth
2017

"**W**ait, you mean now?!" she'd blurted. Peggy had been trying to wrap her head around what was being asked of her.

This wasn't the first conversation she'd had with her friend Senator Ryan Winkler about the possibility of her running for office. Peggy had gotten to know Senator Winkler the year prior to his request, when they worked together on a bill to raise the minimum wage. Senator Winkler authored the bill to raise the state minimum wage to $9.50 per hour, and Peggy pushed to get it through the legislature.

Back then, Peggy was the executive director of CDF, the Children's Defense Fund. It was her job to advocate on behalf of the children of Minnesota. When then-Governor Mark Dayton signed their minimum wage increase into law, it was one of her proudest moments as a child advocate. That increase in minimum wage meant more families would be able to put food on their tables. It meant more kids might not go to bed hungry.

A few years later, Senator Winkler was retiring and moving to Belgium with his family. He wanted Peggy to run for his seat. It was a lot to process. When they'd talked about it before, Peggy always thought they were talking about years in the future. But it was happening much sooner than she'd imagined, and Peggy had a decision to make. All of the things she'd have to figure out started running through her mind: *What about my family? What about my job? Am I even ready for this?*

Peggy knew the answer to the last question, even if she'd had some doubts. She had spent years working for Wellstone Action, an organization dedicated to continuing the work of the late senator. She'd worked for its Camp Wellstone program, training people to run campaigns. Peggy is an expert on campaigns. Still, Senator Winkler's offer was very sudden and Peggy had a lot to think about.

She thought about the work they had done together to get their bill passed. As the director of CDF, Peggy had a platform. But she couldn't author and introduce bills. That was the job of a legislator. As a legislator, Peggy could write more laws to help the families of Minnesota.

As a child advocate to her core, Peggy knew what she needed to do. Peggy ran for and was elected to the Minnesota House of Representatives. She was the first Ojibwe to serve in the House.

Now, Peggy wraps her red and black buffalo plaid coat tighter around herself as she walks to her car. This election, the one she's out there knocking on doors for, is huge. For a third time now, Peggy had been called upon to run for office. This time, it was her friend Tim Walz who was asking her to run. Peggy has known Tim for many years, ever since she was his trainer at Camp Wellstone.

When he had asked to meet with her, Peggy thought she knew what he wanted to talk about. Peggy had heard Tim would be running for governor, and she was happy to give her friend some advice. She told him she thought it would be a good idea for him to choose a running mate from the Twin Cities area, and to pick a woman, especially an Indigenous woman or woman of color.

As it turns out, Tim had the same idea. It had to be Peggy. It wasn't even a question, really. Peggy was absolutely the right person for the job. The *only* person for the job. And so Peggy agreed to run with Tim as lieutenant governor to his governor.

Chapter Nine

THE SECOND MOST POWERFUL PERSON IN MINNESOTA

St. Paul, MN
January 7, 2019

Peggy Flanagan puts her hand on the Bible. Peggy has chosen to swear her oath on a very special Bible, an Ojibwe language Bible. This Bible was written in 1854 and was on loan from the Minnesota Historical Society for this occasion. This Bible is very important to Peggy. It represents two aspects of herself: her identity as an Ojibwe and her identity as a Catholic.

These two parts of Peggy are seemingly at odds with one another. Christianity has often been used as a justification for taking Native lands and for not allowing Natives to practice their own religious beliefs. But being both Ojibwe and Catholic makes Peggy who she is. Peggy has embraced something her mentor told her. She was told to reject the idea of walking in two worlds. Ojibwe women (ikwe) are Ojibwe women all the time. This identity is not something she steps out of when she steps into another role. Rather than walking in two worlds, she walks in one big, complicated, sometimes messy world.

The inauguration is taking place at the historic Fitzgerald Theater in St. Paul. The theater is packed. Peggy was nervous, but mostly excited, when she took the stage. She is so grateful to have the important people in her life with her at her inauguration ceremony.

Her mother is there. Her father traveled all the way from the White Earth Reservation in northern Minnesota to be there.

Peggy is thankful to have both of her parents with her. She knows they are proud of her and all she has accomplished. Peggy is equally proud to be their daughter. Peggy's own daughter, Siobahn, is there at her side. Peggy loves her daughter more than anything in the whole world, and she is so grateful that Siobahn is able to be a part of this historic moment.

Peggy is also grateful that another member of her family, her partner, Tom, is able to be there. Peggy is grateful to have Tom in her life. He makes her laugh. He is supportive. Peggy knows he is very, very proud of her. Peggy knows their bond is strong. Peggy is excited for whatever the future holds for both of them.

Peggy is also excited about all the ways her Native culture and traditions are a part of the inauguration ceremony. The swearing in is being done by Justice McKeig, a fellow Anishinaabekwe, an Ojibwe woman. Justice McKeig was the first Native woman appointed to the Minnesota Supreme Court.

Peggy is wearing traditional clothing for the occasion. She is wearing a beautiful pink ribbon dress. Ribbon dresses and skirts are important ceremonial garments for women of certain Native tribes, such as the Ojibwe. Peggy is also wearing a special beaded medallion. On her feet, Peggy wears makazinag, moccasins.

A representative from the White Earth Nation joined the Minnesota National Guard for the presentation of the colors. A Native drum group played a flag song to honor the veterans. It makes Peggy happy and proud to have her Native heritage play an important role in such an important ceremony.

When she swears her oath, Peggy becomes Lieutenant Governor

Peggy Flanagan. The words that were spoken did something. They made Peggy the second most powerful person in the state of Minnesota. It wasn't something she had set out to accomplish. There was a time, those 1.75 GPA days, when this wasn't even something Peggy could begin to imagine. But with the swearing of the oath, Peggy became Minnesota's fiftieth lieutenant governor and the first-ever Native American woman to hold the office. She also became the highest-ranking Native woman elected to an executive office in the entire United States of America. This is a big deal. It is a huge accomplishment for Peggy, but it is also important for Native Americans everywhere. It is important for Natives to have people in positions of power, so they can advocate for Native people and Native families. Peggy has been that advocate for years. Today will be a big step in Peggy's ongoing journey toward making life better for her people.

All of the days since winning the election in November 2018 have led up to this moment. The year 2018 was big for Native women in politics. The first Native women were elected to Congress: Representatives Sharice Davids and Deb Haaland. Across the country, Native women ran for office in record numbers. While it might seem like the start of a new movement, the movement itself is a return to the traditional. Native women have always been leaders. Now they are taking their skills and running for office. The election of Lieutenant Governor Flanagan opens the door for Native women in politics, and she will use her strength to hold that door open.

As lieutenant governor, Peggy will also provide much-needed representation for Native children. Her being in such an important public position is proof that it is possible for Natives to step into these roles. And her words of encouragement will speak to all the children across Minnesota who may feel like they are unseen or overlooked. Peggy sees them. She knows they are valuable and she will work to help them see their value.

"Let's get to work. Chi miigwech. Thank you," she says.

Peggy has just finished giving her address, her first time speaking as lieutenant governor. It was as much a love letter to the state and people of Minnesota as it was a speech. And Peggy meant every word she said. They were all in this together. They were One Minnesota. Peggy was truly excited to get to work on behalf of the people of Minnesota, the people who inspire her, the people she will never quit fighting for and representing.

Chapter Ten

CEREMONY

Red Wing, MN
September 14, 2019

"**C**heers!"

Glasses are clinking and Peggy Flanagan and Tom Weber's guests are enjoying some amazing local food and beverages. This day could not have been any more perfect. Peggy's friend, Governor Tim Walz, has just finished toasting the happy couple. It's incredible that they were able to pull off such a lovely wedding so quickly. They had a lot of help, and for that they're grateful. Still, people usually take at least a year to plan a wedding and they only had a few months. Peggy and Tom had both been married before, so it wasn't the first wedding for either of them. They just wanted to start their lives together as soon as possible.

Tom had proposed to her in June. Peggy was happy and surprised, and of course she said yes! It wasn't all that long ago, January 2018, that Peggy had made the official announcement on her Facebook page that they were a couple. It's weird having your love life be public business, but it is what it is if one of you is lieutenant governor and the other is a journalist. At the time, Tom had been working for Minnesota Public Radio (MPR). When they announced they were a couple, Tom was unassigned coverage of the governor's race. They didn't want there to be any sense of unfairness in the way Tom covered the campaign.

Their wedding took place on Lake Pepin in Red Wing, at their friends' cabin. Peggy's dress was designed and created for her by Minneapolis fashion designer Samantha Rei, a former contestant on the TV show *Project Runway*. Samantha Rei had also designed Peggy's beautiful plaid dress for her inaugural ball. Peggy knows it is important to support local artists, and women of color in the arts especially.

The dress Samantha Rei designed for her turned out beautifully. Her wedding dress includes traditional Ojibwe elements such as the ribbon skirt. The three ribbons in different shades of blue on Peggy's wedding dress represent Tom, Peggy, and Siobhan. The blue ribbons go perfectly with Tom's blue suit. Peggy also wore a beautiful beaded medallion that once belonged to Senator Wellstone.

As part of their wedding ceremony, Peggy and Tom smudge with sage and participate in a traditional Ojibwe blanket ceremony. The couple stand together, wrapped in a beautiful blanket designed by Ojibwe artist Sarah Agaton Howes.

It is a beautiful day with friends and family. Peggy is excited for her life with Tom. She knows that whatever life might throw at them, they can handle it together.

Chapter Eleven

EVERYTHING IS DIFFERENT NOW

St. Louis Park, MN
March 2020

Peggy Flanagan is at home. Her whole family is at home. The whole state of Minnesota is at home—at least they should be, unless they are working an essential job, like a nurse or a grocery store employee.

Governor Walz has issued a stay-at-home order to stop the spread of the COVID-19 virus. Peggy is proud of the way he is handling this situation. Neither of them had planned on a pandemic when they decided to run for office together. Yet, here they are.

To Minnesota's credit, it's one of the best states in the nation at social distancing. It's not easy convincing people who have been cooped up all winter to remain indoors. Far too many people were unable to resist the urge to flock to the lakes and trails on those first warm spring days. But most people understood that they owe it to each other to stay isolated, so as to not spread the disease to others.

This disease isn't some abstract disaster for Peggy. It is very real. Her brother Ron died of COVID-19. The news reported him as the second person in Tennessee to die from COVID-19. But Ron wasn't just a statistic. He was a brother, a father, a husband, and a friend. He was many things and a good guy, and Peggy still can't believe he's gone.

Ron was her older brother on her father's side. Their father, Marvin Manypenny, died January 26, 2020. It was a tragic loss for

Peggy and for the people of the White Earth Reservation. Marvin was an important activist in the Native community who worked to make things better for Native Americans everywhere. Peggy learned a lot from her father. Although he hadn't been a part of her childhood, Peggy and her father had reconnected after she finished college. She likes to think she got his best years.

Peggy and her father took very different approaches in the way they went about their activism. Not all Native people think alike. The relationship between Native people and the governments of the United States is complicated. People hold different views on how to work within these different systems. Peggy's father saw the government as something to fight. Peggy saw it as a system that might have some flaws, but that had potential to help people. Their different approaches can be summarized as "burn it down or change it from within." Peggy's father took the "burn it down" approach, which can be understandable, given the terrible ways the US government has treated Native people. Peggy has taken the "change it from within" approach. She has been remarkably successful in working within the government to create change for the better. She has used her leadership and position of power to make lives better for Native children and Native families. Despite their differences, Peggy and her father loved each other very much. Marvin Manypenny was very proud of all his daughter accomplished. And Peggy was very proud to be his daughter.

Peggy and her father came from the Ma'iingan, wolf clan. In Ojibwe culture, people inherit their clan designation from their fathers. Peggy belongs to the wolf clan because that is her father's clan. Wolves are protectors. Peggy could always understand where her father was coming from, even if she didn't agree with his methods.

The year 2020 has gotten off to a rough start. Between losing her father and her brother, and this pandemic, Peggy is just grateful she has Tom and Siobhan to stay at home with for weeks. They make the tough times better.

Still, Peggy's first year in office was incredibly productive. She accomplished many important things. Among her most important achievements was the creation of a Missing and Murdered Indigenous Women Task Force. All across the nation, Indigenous women are disappearing and being killed at alarming rates. Minnesota is facing this problem, even more so as pipelines encroach on Native lands. This task force's motto is "Not one more" because it works to identify the causes of this tragedy and to find solutions so not one more Native woman is lost.

The disease COVID-19 is hitting Native people across the country especially hard. The effects of colonialism have left Native people dealing with serious health issues that make them more susceptible to the disease. Some reservations don't have hospitals that can handle a large number of people. Some Native Americans don't even have running water. And in many cases, several generations of a family live together in the same house, leaving no room for anyone to socially distance.

Despite everything, Peggy is optimistic. She has faith in Tim Walz as a leader. She is doing everything she can to help the people of Minnesota through this crisis. Working from home is strange and is taking some getting used to. She misses the capitol and her office. Peggy thinks about her desk and all the hours of work she'd put in there. She has a little placard on her desk that says "What would Beyoncé do?" Peggy suspects this might be one of the few situations that would be a struggle even for Beyoncé. Even though this situation is scary, Peggy knows she has to keep her head in the game and keep working.

No one knows for certain what the future holds. A lot of fictional stories are about the aftermath of a virus outbreak. They are stories about surviving in a new and hostile world. But these stories often leave out what came before. They leave out the sadness of loss and the difficulties of isolation. But that's what we're living with now and Peggy just wants to help everyone get through this safely. She's Ma'iingan. Wolves protect their pack.

Not everything that spreads is bad, like this virus. Across the land, Native people are returning to tradition to deal with the problems of this world. Natives are returning to traditional foods and arts and sciences. They're returning to traditional roles, like Peggy did in becoming a leader for her people. The return to tradition is catching on. It's spreading. More and more Natives are seeing the healing power of tradition.

Peggy carries the wisdom and strength of her people with her. She has devoted herself to making the world a kinder place, not just for Native children and Native families, but for all children and all families. She has shown Native children that they should dream big, that nothing is out of reach. She has shown Native women that they belong in any space they want to be in and that their presence is valuable.

It is possible that one day Peggy will be the first Native woman governor, or the first Native woman president. It is possible that the first Native woman president will say, "I am here today because women like Peggy Flanagan paved the way."

It can be hard for Native children to believe these things are possible. It's difficult to see things as possible if they don't match what you actually see. But now Native kids can see Lieutenant Governor Peggy Flanagan and know that Native American, Ojibwe, and other Indigenous people can have an important role in shaping our future.

EXTEND YOUR LEARNING

The activities and additional information in the following pages are intended for use with the Charles Albert Bender, Ella Cara Deloria, and Peggy Flanagan books in the Minnesota Native Lives Series.

IDEAS FOR WRITING AND DISCUSSION

What Do You Think?

- What moment in this story do you think you will most remember? Why?

- Who do you believe was most important to this person's success? Why?

- What do you think were the hardest moments for this person? Why?

- How do you think this person was able to overcome hardship in their life?

- What were the happiest moments in the story of this person's life?

- What are some of the happiest moments in your life?

- What moment in the story reminded you of something in your own life?

- Write your own short autobiography, the story of your life so far, told by you!

IDEAS FOR VISUAL PROJECTS

Show Us What You Think

- Draw images for three or four moments that are not illustrated in this book.

- Draw a sketch of this person and include items they liked.

- Find images from American Indian Boarding Schools from the time this book covers.

- Find historic images to share of activities the book mentions. Are they different now?

- Find historic images to share of the reservations or places the book mentions.

- Make a map of the eleven tribal nations within the boundaries of the state of Minnesota. Where are they located? What tribe lives there? What else did you learn?

- Give a visual presentation on how treaties formed the White Earth Reservation, homeland of both Charles Albert Bender amd Peggy Flanagan. Explore "Why Treaties Matter" for information.

- Create a bar graph or pie chart or other infographic on one of these topics:

  1. How many Native Americans live in urban areas of Minnesota? Which cities in Minnesota are home to the largest populations of Native Americans?

  2. Many Native American students attend school in Minnesota—you may be one of them. How many Native American students are in your school district? How many tribes are represented?

Resources

- Minnesota Indian Education—Teaching and Learning: www.education.mn.gov/MDE/dse/indian/teach

- Why Treaties Matter: www.treatiesmatter.org/exhibit/ wp-content/uploads/2017/09/Updated-Sovereign-Nations1.pdf

IDEAS FOR FURTHER LEARNING

Dakota and Ojibwe people continue to live in Minnesota and are part of all aspects of our society. While English is a shared language, many Dakota and Ojibwe people also study and speak their Indigenous languages called Dakota and Anishinaabemowin.

Find Out More

- Find unfamiliar words in this book and create a glossary or word list with their definitions.

- Create a timeline for this person's life. Add dates from the timeline on page 53.

- Learn how to count to ten in Dakota or Ojibwe.

- Look up Ojibwe or Dakota words for baseball or ball games such as lacrosse.

- Learn about Dakota and Ojibwe sports and activities, such as powwows.

- Make a list of four common traditions the Ojibwe and Dakota share.

Resources

- Ojibwe People's Dictionary: ojibwe.lib.umn.edu

- Beginning Dakota: www.beginningdakota.org

- In Honor of the People: www.inhonorofthepeople.org

- Minnesota Historical Society, Minnesota Territory:
  www.mnhs.org/talesoftheterritory

- Ojibwe Material Culture:
  www.mnhs.org/ojibwematerialculture

- Oceti Sakowiŋ, The Seven Council Fires:
  www.mnhs.org/sevencouncilfires

Historical Context

Dakota and Ojibwe people live in today's context of the twenty-first century. We also have histories as rich and full of struggle as the US or other countries. This timeline presents important events in one place as a reminder that no one human history is more important than another, but history often makes it look that way. This timeline also provides context from Dakota and Ojibwe history. You can use it to respond to the books in this series by comparing each person's timeline and history to the events listed here.

Beyond memory, this place called Mni Sota Makoce, or Minnesota, is where the people became Dakota. They traveled as far north as Hudson Bay, as far west as the Rocky Mountains, south to trade with the Pueblos, and past the trading city of Cahokia, to the southeastern part of what later became the United States.

During this same time, Anishinaabeg, the larger group that includes Ojibwe people, lived far to the east of Minnesota, near the Atlantic Ocean. A series of prophecies, or visions of their future, set the Ojibwe off on their five-hundred-year journey to find a new home in "a land where food grows on water" (meaning manoomin, wild rice) along the Great Lakes and eventually in Minnesota.

TIMELINE

900	Dakota live, as they have always, in what will become Minnesota; ancestors of the Ojibwe begin migrating west to find a new homeland that was foretold in a vision.
1400	Ancestors of the Ojibwe reach the northwestern area of what later becomes Minnesota.
1540s	Spanish explorers map the Mississippi River and Dakota village sites.
1622	Ojibwe make contact with French explorer Étienne Brûlé at Lake Superior.
1689	Ojibwe fight for the French against the British until 1763 in what is now the US and Canada.
1730s	Ojibwe and Dakota begin battles over Dakota territories that end in the 1850s.
1769	Dartmouth College is founded to educate Native Americans in Christian theology.
1783	The American Revolution ends.
1805	Zebulon Pike and Dakota sign an agreement to sell land to the Americans in present-day Minneapolis. The Dakota are never paid for the land.

1812	Ojibwe and Dakota fight on the side of the British in the War of 1812.
1816	Saswe, Ella Cara Deloria's grandfather, is born in what is now Minnesota.
1819	Americans build a fort at Bdote (where the rivers meet in present-day St. Paul).
1825	Dakota and Ojibwe leaders and other tribes sign the Prairie du Chien Treaty and lose their land.
1830	Congress passes the Indian Removal Act. All Native Americans are required to move west of the Mississippi River. Many tribes remain in their homelands. Some are marched by force hundreds of miles from their homelands.
1837	A series of treaties begins where both Dakota and Ojibwe peoples' lands are taken away and many are forced to move.
1849	Minnesota Territory begins a period of organization (claiming) by the US that lasts until 1858.
1850s	Treaties require Dakota and Ojibwe to let go of hundreds of millions of acres of land.
1853	The 1851 treaties are ratified; American settlers encroach on Dakota lands.
1858	Minnesota becomes a state.
1858	Pay shah de o quay/Mary Razor, mother of Charles Albert Bender, is born.
1861	The American Civil War begins.

1862	War between the Dakota and the US begins in August. The fighting lasts six weeks.
1862	The Dakota ask the Ojibwe to protect their big drum during the war with the US.
1863	Treaties with Dakota people are repealed and almost all Dakota are removed from Minnesota.
1865	The American Civil War ends.
1867	The White Earth Reservation is established.
1870	Dakota and Ojibwe sign a peace treaty that remains unbroken.
1879	Colonel Richard Pratt founds the Carlisle Indian Boarding School.
1880s	Dakota people return to their communities in Minnesota.
1884	Charles Albert Bender is born in Brainerd, Minnesota.
1884	The Haskell Institute opens as a boarding school for Native American children.
1889	Ella Cara Deloria is born on the Yankton Reservation in South Dakota.
1902	Charles Albert Bender graduates from the Carlisle Indian School in Pennsylvania.
1914	Ella Cara Deloria graduates from Columbia University with a bachelor's degree in education.
1924	The Indian Citizenship Act of Congress grants citizenship to all Native Americans.

1925	Charles Albert Bender retires from professional baseball.
1932	Ella Cara Deloria publishes *Dakota Texts*.
1934	The Indian Reorganization Act is passed, forcing tribes to all operate by the same government model.
1944	Ella Cara Deloria publishes *Speaking of Indians*.
1953	Charles Albert Bender is inducted into the National Baseball Hall of Fame.
1953	The Termination Resolution by Congress is passed, intending to end US recognition of tribes.
1954	Charles Albert Bender dies in Pennsylvania.
1956	The Indian Relocation Act is passed to move Native Americans off reservations and into cities.
1971	Ella Cara Deloria dies in South Dakota.
1978	The Religious Freedom Act is passed, ending laws against religious and cultural practices of tribes.
1979	Peggy Flanagan is born in St. Louis Park, Minnesota.
1988	Ella Cara Deloria's *Waterlily* is published.
2007	Ella Cara Deloria's *The Dakota Way of Life* is published.
2019	Peggy Flanagan is sworn in as lieutenant governor of Minnesota, making her the highest-ranking Native American woman elected to an executive office in the United States.

ABOUT THE AUTHOR

Jessica Engelking is the daughter of an enrolled member of the White Earth Band of Ojibwe. She grew up in Warroad, Minnesota, with her parents and younger sister. After high school, she attended the University of Minnesota–Morris, making use of their American Indian Tuition Waiver. She graduated with a BA in philosophy and went on to study philosophy at the graduate level. She received her MA in philosophy from the University of Iowa. Jessica liked Iowa City so much that she stayed there a few years after she was done with school. She moved back to Minnesota and lived for a short time in Ely. Jessica loved living so close to the Boundary Waters. She then moved in with her sister and niece so she could help out, as aunties do. She currently resides in Minnetonka and is isolating in Elkader, Iowa, with her boyfriend, David, and dog, Walden. She is working from home as the social media manager for the Great Plains Action Society, a Native nonprofit. Jessica enjoys running with her dog, spending time on the water, reading, and she's trying to get better at beading.

ABOUT THE ILLUSTRATOR

Tashia Hart grew up in the wilds of Minnesota. She loves animals, writing, drawing, plants, and cooking. She is the author of *Gidjie and the Wolves* (Intermediaries, volume 1) and *Girl Unreserved* (Broken Wings and Things, volume 1). Her forthcoming wild rice cookbook, in partnership with the Minnesota Historical Society Press, is set to be released in the fall of 2021. She writes essays and recipes about wild foods for various organizations and tribal programs, and is an avid beader with thirty years of experience. She believes Indigenous people should control how their stories and likenesses are portrayed, and so has recently started the independent publishing company (Not) Too Far Removed Press. The mission of the press is to uplift fellow Indigenous authors and artists of the Midwest region. Tashia is Red Lake Anishinaabe. www.tashiahart.com

ABOUT THE SERIES EDITORS

Heid E. Erdrich is Ojibwe enrolled at the Turtle Mountain Reservation in North Dakota. She grew up in Wahpeton, North Dakota, not far from the White Earth Reservation in Minnesota and the Sisseton-Wahpeton Reservation in South Dakota. Her neighbors in her hometown were Dakota and Ojibwe from these tribal nations. Heid is the author of seven collections of poetry and a cookbook focused on indigenous foods of Minnesota and neighboring states titled *Original Local*. Her writing has won fellowships and awards from the National Poetry Series, Native Arts and Cultures Foundation, Minnesota State Arts Board, and more. She has twice won a Minnesota Book Award for poetry. A longtime teacher of writing at colleges and universities, Heid enjoys editing. She edited the anthologies *New Poets of Native Nations* from Graywolf Press, and *Sister Nations* from the Minnesota Historical Society Press. Heid's new poetry collection is *Little Big Bully*, Penguin Editions, 2020. Along with being Anishinaabe/Ojibwe, Heid's extended family includes Anishinaabe from several bands, Dakota, Hidatsa, Somali American, German American, and immigrants from India and elsewhere. She is also Metis, a group of people whose ancestors were French and Native American, and who lived in what became the United States and Canada. She loves the Great Lakes area and calls it home. Heid has lived in Minnesota for many years, raising her kids in Minneapolis, where they went to public schools. She enjoyed working with the authors and editors of this series of biographies and hopes you will read and reread these books!

Gwen Nell Westerman is Dakota and enrolled with the Sisseton Wahpeton Oyate in South Dakota. She is also a citizen of the Cherokee Nation. Her parents went to boarding schools in Oklahoma and South Dakota, and met at the Haskell Institute in Lawrence, Kansas. Gwen grew up in Oklahoma and Kansas among many different tribal nations. One of her earliest memories is when she was three, scribbling in a book. Her mother asked what she was doing and Gwen said, "I'm writing!" Today, she writes about Dakota history and language. She has won two Minnesota Book Awards for her work about Dakota people. Gwen's first poetry book was written in English and Dakota. Her poems have been published in anthologies, and so have her art quilts. Her quilt art received awards from the Minnesota State Arts Board, the Minnesota Historical Society, the Great Plains Art Museum, and the Heard Museum, and has been exhibited in many places across the United States. Her children were born in Oklahoma and grew up in Minnesota. Gwen's family tree includes teachers, leaders, and hard workers who were Dakota, Ojibwe, Odawa, and Cherokee, along with a few French and Scottish traders. She knows the names of all her ancestors on both sides of her family back before the American Revolution. She lives in Minnesota with her husband and their little black dog. She hopes you enjoy reading these books as much as she liked working on them, and that you will share them with your friends and families.